PUFFIN BOOKS

James and the Giant Peach: A Play

Roald Dahl was born in 1916 in Wales of Norwegian parents. He was educated in England before starting work for the Shell Oil Company in Africa. He began writing after a 'monumental bash on the head' sustained as an RAF fighter pilot during the Second World War. Roald Dahl is one of the most successful and well known of all children's writers. His books, which are read by children the world over, include *James and the Giant Peach*, *Charlie and the Chocolate Factory*, *The Magic Finger*, *Charlie and the Great Glass Elevator*, *Fantastic Mr Fox*, *Matilda*, *The Twits*, *The BFG* and *The Witches*, winner of the 1983 Whitbread Award. Roald Dahl died in 1990 at the age of seventy-four.

ROALD DAHL'S

# James
## and the
# Giant Peach:
# A Play

✳ ✳ ✳ ✳ ✳ ✳ ✳ ✳

Adapted by Richard George

Introduction by Roald Dahl

PUFFIN BOOKS

Find out more about Roald Dahl
by visiting the web site at
# www.roalddahl.com

PUFFIN BOOKS

Published by the Penguin Group
Penguin Books Ltd, 80 Strand, London, WC2R 0RL, England
Penguin Putnam Inc., 375 Hudson Street, New York, New York 10014, USA
Penguin Books Australia Ltd, Ringwood, Victoria, Australia
Penguin Books Canada Ltd, 10 Alcorn Avenue, Toronto, Ontario, Canada M4V 3B2
Penguin Books India (P) Ltd, 11 Community Centre, Panchsheel Park, New Delhi – 110 017, India
Penguin Books (NZ) Ltd, Cnr Rosedale and Airborne Roads, Albany, Auckland, New Zealand
Penguin Books (South Africa) (Pty) Ltd, 24 Sturdee Avenue, Rosebank 2196, South Africa

Penguin Books Ltd, Registered Offices: 80 Strand, London, WC2R 0RL, England

www.penguin.com

First published 1982
21

Set in Monophoto Baskerville

Printed in England by Clays Ltd, St Ives plc

British Library Cataloguing in Publication Data
A CIP catalogue record for this book is available from the British Library

ISBN 0–140–31464–4

# CONTENTS

*James and the Giant Peach* was my first book for children. I wrote it during the winter of 1960–61 in New York, and I started it because I wanted to attempt something different after seventeen years of writing nothing but short stories for adults.

I can remember vividly that I was sitting at my desk and playing around with the lines of 'The Centipede's Song' when my wife burst into the room and told me that our son Theo, then three months old, had been hit by a taxi-cab while out in his pram with his nurse. I dropped my pencil and we both rushed to the hospital. His head injuries were severe and almost fatal, and the next few months were desperate times, with brain operations and endless journeys through the snow to hospital, and all the awful tensions that grip a mother and father when they are fighting to save their baby's life.

When you are writing fantasy, which is a very different thing from writing fiction, you must be able, the moment you pick up the pencil, to shut out all normal surroundings and go flying away to a magic world where everything is enchanting and fantastic. You must lose sight of the room you are sitting in and you must become deaf to all noises outside your window. Quite honestly, you must go into a sort of trance. (That's why you never think about the story you are working on except when you are at your desk and the dream-world is upon you.)

I was able to switch off like this for about three hours a day during the fearful Theo crisis, and I found that it actually rested me and helped me to retain my sanity during those months. Thus I finished *James* and delivered it to the publisher before the winter was out, and long before Theo had had his last brain operation.

I know from the letters I get that many schools like to make plays from my children's books. The excellent adaptation of *Charlie and the Chocolate Factory* by the American school teacher, Richard George, has been well received by teachers and children in several countries, and I believe that the splendid job he has done here on *James and the Giant Peach* will be equally useful.

It is lovely to know that, after twenty-one years, not only my son Theo but also *James* are both still very much alive.

ROALD DAHL

# JAMES AND
# THE GIANT PEACH

## CAST OF CHARACTERS
### (In order of appearance)

Mother
Father
Narrator
Aunt Sponge
Aunt Spiker
James Trotter
Little Old Man
Crowd Member
Old-Green-Grasshopper
Silkworm
Centipede
Spider
Ladybird
Earthworm
Glow-worm
Captain
First Officer
Second Officer
Cloud-Men
Onlookers
Passengers

## SCENE 1

*James Henry Trotter's* FATHER *and* MOTHER *come running through the curtain as if chased by something . . . running in place after appearing on audience-side of curtain.*

MOTHER: Ohhhhh . . . I don't believe it! I just . . . don't believe it! Help . . . Help, somebody!

FATHER: Hurry, Mrs Trotter! Hurry!

MOTHER: Ohhh . . . can't we sit down and rest?

FATHER: *Rest?* When an escaped rhinoceros is trying to eat us up?

MOTHER: But I am tired.

FATHER: Don't be ridiculous . . . It's gaining on us! Hurry!

MOTHER: I don't think we're going to make it, Mr Trotter!

FATHER: No, neither do I! Well . . . good-bye Mrs Trotter.

MOTHER: Good-bye, Mr Trottttttteeeeeeeeerrrr. [*Fading out*]

[*They run as if going forwards but really go back-
wards behind and through the curtain to give impression of being swallowed up*]

NARRATOR: *Wow!* What a beginning to a story! Can
you believe that? Well . . . I'm sorry we have to
start this story with such a terrible event as a
mother and father being swallowed up by an
escaped rhinoceros, but I just *had* to tell you. It's
because of this event that this story happened. You
see, life was really great for our hero, James Henry
Trotter . . . until this . . . happened to his parents.
Now . . . well . . . he was sent away to live with his
two aunts, Aunt Sponge and Aunt Spiker. I am
sorry to point out, but I must, that they were both
really *horrible* people. They were selfish and lazy
and cruel, and right from the beginning they
started beating poor James for almost *no* reason at
all. They never called him by his real name, but
always referred to him as 'you miserable creature',
or 'you disgusting little beast', or 'you filthy nuis-
ance', and they certainly never gave him any toys
to play with or any picture books to look at or
read. His room was as bare as a prison cell. They
lived – Aunt Sponge, Aunt Spiker, and now James
as well – in a queer, ramshackle house on the
top of a high hill in the South of England. The hill
was so high that from almost anywhere in the

garden James could look down and see for miles and miles across a marvellous landscape of woods and fields; and on a *very clear day*, if he looked in the right direction, he could see a tiny grey dot far away on the horizon, which was the house that he used to live in with his beloved mother and father. And just beyond that, he could see the sea itself – a long, thin streak of blackish-blue, like a line of ink, beneath the rim of the sky. But then, there came a morning when something rather peculiar happened to him. It all started on a blazing hot day in the middle of summer. Aunt Sponge, Aunt Spiker, and James were all out in the garden. James had been put to work, as usual. This time he was chopping wood for the kitchen stove. Aunt Sponge and Aunt Spiker were sitting comfortably in deck-chairs near by, sipping tall glasses of fizzy lemonade and watching him to see that he didn't stop work for one moment. Let's take a closer look at what's happening. [*Fade out*]

[*Curtain opens*]

AUNT SPONGE:

I look and smell, I do declare, as lovely as a rose!
Just feast your eyes upon my face, observe my shapely nose!
Behold my heavenly silky locks!

And if I take off both my socks
You'll see my dainty toes.

AUNT SPIKER:

But don't forget, my old dear Sponge, how much
your tummy shows!

Why, Sponge . . . you're red. Go soak your head
. . . my sweet, you cannot win.
Behold my gorgeous curvy shape, my teeth, my
charming grin!
Oh, beauteous me! How I adore
My radiant looks! And please ignore
The pimple on my chin.

AUNT SPONGE:

My dear old trout! To the world I'll shout . . .
YOU'RE ONLY BONES AND SKIN!

Such loveliness as I possess can only truly shine
In Hollywood! I do declare. Oh, wouldn't that be
fine!
I'd capture all the nations' hearts!
They'd give me all the leading parts!
The stars would all resign!

AUNT SPIKER:

I think you'd make, without mistake . . . a lovely
Frankenstein.

[JAMES *begins to act very tired and sweaty – almost as if he's going to faint*]
What's the matter with you?

JAMES: Gee, Aunt Spiker . . . I feel . . . as if I'm . . . going to . . . going to . . . going to faint . . .

AUNT SPONGE: Stop that immediately and get on with your work, you nasty little beast!

JAMES: Oh, Auntie Sponge! And Auntie Spiker! Couldn't we all – please – just for once – go down to the seaside on the bus? It isn't far – and I feel so hot and awful and lonely . . .

AUNT SPIKER: [*Shouting*] WHY, YOU LAZY, GOOD-FOR-NOTHING BRUTE!

AUNT SPONGE: [*Yelling*] BEAT HIM!

AUNT SPIKER: I certainly will! [*Glaring at* JAMES] I shall beat you later on in the day when I don't feel so hot. And now get out of my sight, *you disgusting little worm*, and give me some peace!
[JAMES *backs up in a frightened manner and everyone freezes*]

NARRATOR: It was at this point that the first thing, the rather peculiar thing, happened to James.
[JAMES *acts as if he hears something rustling in the bushes behind him. The two* AUNTS *can either move*

*off stage or take frozen-action positions.* LITTLE
OLD MAN *appears from behind bushes*]

LITTLE OLD MAN: Come closer to me, little boy.
Come right up close to me, and I will show you
something wonderful.
[*The* OLD MAN *hobbles a step or two nearer, and
then he puts a hand into the pocket of his jacket and
takes out a small, white paper bag*]

LITTLE OLD MAN: [*Whispering*] You see this? [*Waving
the bag in front of* JAMES's *face*] You know what this
is, my dear? You know what's inside this little bag?
[*He comes still closer to* JAMES, *so close that he is only a
few inches away*] Take a look, my dear. [*Opening the
bag and letting* JAMES *look inside*] *Listen* to them!
Listen to them move! There's more power and
magic in these little green things than in all the
rest of the world put together.

JAMES: But – but – what are they? [*Pause*] Where do
they come from?

LITTLE OLD MAN: Ah-ha . . . you'd never guess that!
[*Suddenly the* OLD MAN *jumps back and begins waving
his stick madly in the air*] Crocodile tongues! One
thousand long, slimy crocodile tongues boiled up
in the skull of a dead witch for twenty days and
nights with the eyeballs of a lizard! Add the fingers
of a young monkey, the gizzard of a pig, the beak

of a green parrot, the juice of a porcupine, and three spoonfuls of sugar. Stew for another week, and then let the moon do the rest! [*All at once, he pushes the white paper bag into* JAMES'*s hands*] *Here.* You take it! It's *yours*! [*Pause*] And now, all you've got to do is this. Take a large jug of water, and pour all the little green things into it. Then, very slowly, one by one, add ten hairs from your own head. That sets them off! In a couple of minutes the water will begin to froth and bubble furiously, and as soon as that happens you must quickly drink it all down, the whole jugful, in one gulp. And *then*, my dear, you will feel it churning and boiling in your stomach, and steam will start coming out of your mouth, and immediately after that, *marvellous* things will start happening to you, *fabulous*, *unbelievable* things – and you will never be miserable again in your life. Because you *are* miserable, aren't you? You needn't tell me! I know all about it! Now, off you go and do exactly as I say. Don't let those green things in there get away from you. Because if they do escape, then they will be working their magic upon somebody else instead of upon you! *Whoever they meet first, be it bug, insect, animal, or tree, that will be the one who gets the full power of their magic!* So, hold the bag tight! Off you go! Hurry up! Don't wait! Now's the time! Hurry!

[OLD MAN *turns and slips away into the bushes.* JAMES *turns and runs towards the house excitedly. He trips under the old peach tree and everything supposedly falls out of the bag*]

JAMES: *Oh, no!* What am I going to do? [*On hands and knees*] Well . . . I suppose I'll just try to pick them . . . *Wait a minute!* They're . . . why . . . why . . . they're burrowing into the ground! I can't seem to get them! *I can't get them!* [*Pause*] They're gone. They're *all gone!* [*He acts very sad and dejected*] But where have they gone to? There's nothing down there except the roots of the old peach tree . . . and a whole lot of earthworms and centipedes and other kinds of insects.

AUNT SPIKER: [*Entering shouting*] GET UP AT ONCE, YOU LAZY LITTLE BEAST! Get back over there immediately and finish chopping up those logs!

AUNT SPONGE: [*Waddling in*] Why don't we just lower the boy down the well in a bucket and leave him there for the night? That ought to teach him not to laze around like this the whole day long.

AUNT SPIKER: That's a very good idea, my dear Sponge. But let's make him finish chopping up the wood first. Be off with you at once, you hideous brat, and do some work!

[JAMES *slowly and sadly gets up and goes back to the wood-pile to begin chopping again*]

AUNT SPIKER: Sponge! Sponge! Come here at once and look at this!

AUNT SPONGE: At what?

AUNT SPIKER: A peach! Right up there on the highest branch! Can't you see it?

AUNT SPONGE: You're teasing me, Spiker. You're making my mouth water on purpose when there's nothing to put into it. Why, that tree's never even had a blossom on it, let alone a peach.

AUNT SPIKER: There's one on it now, Sponge! You look for yourself!

AUNT SPONGE: Very funny ... Ha, ha ... Good gracious me! There really is a peach up there!
[*Everyone takes brief frozen-action position*]

NARRATOR: Now, it's at this point in our story that James feels that something peculiar is about to happen at any moment.
[*Everyone returns to normal action*]

AUNT SPONGE: Hey, you! [*Looking at* JAMES] Come over here at once and climb this tree! I want you to pick that peach up there on the highest branch. Can you see it? [*Pause*]

JAMES: Yes, Auntie Sponge, I can see it.

AUNT SPONGE: And don't you dare to eat any of it yourself. Your Aunt Spiker and I are going to have it between us right here and now, half each. Get on with you! *Up you go!*

AUNT SPIKER: *Stop!* Hold everything! *Look!* Look, Sponge, look!!!

AUNT SPONGE: What's the matter with you?

AUNT SPIKER: It's *growing*! *It's getting bigger and bigger!*

AUNT SPONGE: What is?

AUNT SPIKER: The peach, of course!

AUNT SPONGE: But, my dear Spiker, that's perfectly ridiculous. That's impossible. That's – that's – that's – No – No – that can't be right – No – Yes – Great Scott! The thing really *is* growing!

AUNT SPIKER: Great Caesar's Ghost! I can actually see the thing bulging and swelling before my very eyes!
> [*Everyone just stares as the peach grows by increasing the size of the spotlight on the curtain*]

AUNT SPONGE: Will it ever stop growing? [*Waving her fat arms about*]

AUNT SPIKER: Get away from that tree trunk, you stupid boy! The slightest shake and it will fall off and break.

AUNT SPONGE: Stand back! The branch is bending right down! I can't believe it, but the branch isn't breaking!
   [*The peach is enlarged to a very big size on the curtain*]

AUNT SPIKER: Hallelujah! What a peach!

AUNT SPONGE: Terrifico! Magnifico! Splendifico! And what a meal! [*The two* AUNTS *act as if they are inspecting the peach*] It's ripe! It's just perfect! Now, see here, Spiker. Why don't we go and get us a shovel right away and dig out a great big hunk of it for you and me to eat?

AUNT SPIKER: No, not yet.

AUNT SPONGE: But I can't *wait* to eat some!

AUNT SPIKER: My dear Sponge, there's a pile of money to be made out of this if only we can handle it right. You wait and see.

*End of Scene 1*

## SCENE 2

*Scene can begin in front of stage with curtain closed.* AUNTS *are collecting money from the many onlookers who are curious. There is a fence around the peach area to keep the people out.*

AUNT SPIKER: Roll up! Roll up! Only ten pence to see the Giant Peach!

AUNT SPONGE: Half price for children under two weeks old!

AUNT SPIKER: One at a time, please! Don't push! Don't push! You're all going to get in! [*Many people crowd around with enthusiasm*] Hey, you! Come back, there! You haven't paid!

AUNT SPONGE: It'll cost you double to bring in a camera!

CROWD MEMBER: All right! All right! We don't care!

AUNT SPONGE: [*To* SPIKER] Aren't you glad we put bars on that James's window?

AUNT SPIKER: That disgusting little brute would only get in our way if we let him wander about.

AUNT SPONGE: Can you believe that he complained

that he was lonely, just because he hasn't met any other children for years and years?

AUNT SPIKER: What a nerve! Here we are, just about to become millionaires, and the only thing he can think of is himself!

AUNT SPONGE: Gee, everybody has gone home. Maybe we should close up for tonight, Spiker.

AUNT SPIKER: Maybe you're right, Sponge! We'll get the brat to clean up the mess out here!

AUNT SPONGE: He'll probably want something to eat, since he hasn't had anything all day!

AUNT SPIKER: Well, he'd better not ask! We're too busy to make food! We have to count our money! I'd better call him, to make sure the worm isn't asleep! *Creep! Brat! Wake up, twerp! We have something for you to do immediately!*
 [AUNTS *walk off stage and, after a very brief pause,* JAMES *walks out on the stage alone with very little lighting*]

JAMES: Gee, it really is dark out here tonight. I don't even hear a sound. It's strangely quiet. Boy, am I hungry. I suppose I should be more considerate of my aunts, though. Aunt Spiker says that all I do is think of myself. Maybe she's right. Gee, it's kind of spooky.

NARRATOR: Can you imagine how James feels right now? Have you ever been out alone on a dark, quiet night? Well ... here ... is where James knows (he can just feel it in his bones) that *something stranger than ever* this time, is about to happen to him again. He's sure of it. He can feel it coming.

JAMES: Everything is so *different*. [*Walking and looking around*] Suddenly the whole place seems to be alive with magic. [JAMES *walk towards the Giant Peach and climbs the fence that surrounds it*] Wow, it feels soft and warm! Hmmmmmmmm ... it's a little furry, like the skin of a baby mouse. [*He reaches out and touches it. Suddenly, he notices that, right beside him and below him, there is a hole in the side of the Peach*] What's that? I ... I ... I don't believe it ... but there's ... there's a hole in the side. [*Examines it*] It's quite a large hole, the sort of thing an animal about the size of a fox might make. [JAMES *kneels down and crawls inside, which means through the curtain, continuing to talk as though in a tunnel, using the microphone backstage*] This isn't just a hole, it's a tunnel! Boy! it really is damp and murky in here. These walls are wet and sticky, and it tastes like peach juice dripping from the ceiling. Ummmmm ... delicious! Now it's going uphill, towards the very centre. [*There is now a loud knock as he hits his head*] Ouch! What's this? It seems like a solid wall. It feels like wood, except that it's very jagged and full of deep grooves. Good grief! I know what this is! I've come to the stone in the middle of the Peach! And here . . . is what appears to be a small door cut into the face of the stone. Let's see now . . . uhhh . . . there . . . it swung open. What's this light . . .?

OLD-GREEN-GRASSHOPPER: Look who's here!

CENTIPEDE: We've been waiting for you!

JAMES: Oh no! No! [JAMES *acts scared to death and frozen with fear as the curtain opens slowly to reveal* OLD-GREEN-GRASSHOPPER, SPIDER, LADYBIRD, CENTIPEDE, *and* EARTHWORM *sitting comfortably.* SILKWORM *is curled up asleep in a corner*]

SPIDER: I'm hungry!

OLD-GREEN-GRASSHOPPER: I'm famished!

LADYBIRD: So am I!

CENTIPEDE: Everyone's famished! We need food!
    [*Pause, as all look at* JAMES]

SPIDER: [*Leaning toward* JAMES] Aren't you hungry?
    [JAMES *is still petrified with fear*]

OLD-GREEN-GRASSHOPPER: [*To* JAMES] What's the matter with you? You look positively ill!

CENTIPEDE: He looks as though he's going to faint any second.

LADYBIRD: Oh, my goodness, the poor thing! I do believe he thinks it's *him* that we are wanting to eat! [*Everyone roars with laughter*]

ALL: Oh, dear, oh dear! What an awful thought!

LADYBIRD: You mustn't be frightened. We wouldn't *dream* of hurting you. You are one of us now, didn't you know that? You are one of the crew. We're all in the same boat.

OLD-GREEN-GRASSHOPPER: We've been waiting for you all day long. We thought you were never going to turn up. I'm glad you made it.

CENTIPEDE: So, cheer up, my boy, cheer up! And meanwhile I wish you'd come over here and give me a hand with these boots. It takes me hours to get them all off by myself.
[JAMES *crosses the room and kneels beside* CEN-TIPEDE]

CENTIPEDE: Thank you so much. You are very kind.

JAMES: Well . . . uh . . . you have a lot of boots.

CENTIPEDE: I have a lot of legs and a lot of feet. One hundred, to be exact. [*Proudly*] I *am* a cen-tipede, you know.

EARTHWORM: *There* he goes again! He simply cannot stop telling lies about his legs! He's only got forty-two! The trouble is that most people don't bother to count them. And anyway, there is nothing *marvellous*, you know, Centipede, about having a lot of legs.

CENTIPEDE: Poor Earthworm. [*Whispering in* JAMES'S *ear*] He's blind, you know. He can't see how splendid I look.

EARTHWORM: In my opinion, the *really* marvellous thing is to have no legs at all and to be able to walk just the same.

CENTIPEDE: You call that *walking*! You're a *slitherer*, that's all you are! You just *slither* along.

EARTHWORM: I *glide*.

CENTIPEDE: You are a slimy beast.

EARTHWORM: I am *not* a slimy beast. I am a useful and much-loved creature. Ask any gardener you like. And as for you . . .

CENTIPEDE: I am a *pest*! [*Grinning proudly and looking round the room for approval*]

LADYBIRD: He is *so* proud of that, though for the life of me I cannot understand why. Oh . . . please excuse me . . . my name is Ladybird.

JAMES: Pleased to meet . . .

CENTIPEDE: I am the only pest in this room! Unless you count Old-Green-Grasshopper over there. But he is too old to be a pest any more.

OLD-GREEN-GRASSHOPPER: [*Ignoring* CENTIPEDE] Young fellow, I am Grasshopper, who is rather old, but not a pest. I am a musician.

SPIDER: Well said, Old-Green-Grasshopper! In case you haven't guessed by now, my name is Spider!

CENTIPEDE: James! Your name is James, isn't it?

JAMES: Yes.

CENTIPEDE: Well, James, have you ever in your life seen such a marvellous colossal centipede as me?

JAMES: I certainly haven't! How on earth did you get to be like that?

CENTIPEDE: *Very* peculiar. *Very*, *very* peculiar indeed. I was messing about in the garden under the old peach tree and suddenly a funny little green thing came wriggling past my nose . . .

JAMES: Oh, but I know what that was!

LADYBIRD: It happened to me, too!

SPIDER: And me! Suddenly there were little green things everywhere! The soil was full of them!

EARTHWORM: I actually swallowed one!

LADYBIRD: So did I!

CENTIPEDE: I swallowed three! But who's telling this story anyway? Don't interrupt!

OLD-GREEN-GRASSHOPPER: Not now, Centipede! Why don't you get to the top and get started!
[CENTIPEDE *waddles towards top of peach-light*]

JAMES: What's going on?

SPIDER: In case you don't know it, we are about to depart from the top of this ghastly hill that we've all been living on for so long. We are about to roll away inside this great big beautiful Peach to a land of ... of ... of ... of ... to a land of –

JAMES: Of what?

LADYBIRD: Never you mind! But nothing could be worse than this desolate hilltop and those two repulsive aunts of yours –

ALL: Hear, hear! Hear, hear!

OLD-GREEN-GRASSHOPPER: You may not have noticed it, but the whole garden, even before it reaches the steep edge of the hill, happens to be on a steep slope. And therefore the only thing that has been stopping this Peach from rolling away right from the beginning is the thick stem attaching it to the tree. Break the stem, and off we go!

CENTIPEDE: I've done it! We're off! The journey begins!

EARTHWORM: And who knows where it will end, if *you* have anything to do with it. It can only mean trouble.

LADYBIRD: Nonsense! We are now about to visit the most marvellous places and see the most wonderful things. Isn't that so, Centipede?

CENTIPEDE: There is no knowing what we shall see!

We may see a Creature with forty-nine heads
Who lives in the desolate snow,
And whenever he catches a cold (which he
    dreads)
He has forty-nine noses to blow.

We may see a Dragon, and nobody knows
That we won't see a Unicorn there.
We may see a terrible Monster with toes
Growing out of the tufts of his hair.

We may see the sweet little Biddy-Bright Hen
So playful, so kind, and well bred;
And such beautiful eggs! You just boil them and
    then

They explode and they blow off your head.

But who cares! Let us go from this horrible hill!
Let us roll! Let us bowl! Let us plunge!
Let's go rolling and bowling and spinning until
We're away from old Spiker and Sponge!

*End of Scene 2*

## SCENE 3

AUNTS *are standing outside of closed curtain waiting for the people to come so that they can make more money. Peach-light is on.*

AUNT SPONGE: Why did we have to get up so early, Spiker? Why . . . it's still dark outside.

AUNT SPIKER: Well . . . if an early bird catches the worm, then two early aunts will catch the suckers . . . ha . . . ha . . . ha . . .

AUNT SPONGE: Ha . . . ha . . . ha . . . that's funny . . . ha . . . ha . . . [*Pause*] I . . . don't . . . get it, Spiker! What do you mean?

AUNT SPIKER: Money! We're out here to make money, Sponge! Get it? Make money! M-O-N-E-Y! We shall make a fortune today. Just look at all those people coming up the hill!

AUNT SPONGE: I wonder what became of that horrid little boy of ours last night? He never did come back in, did he?

AUNT SPIKER: He probably fell down in the dark and broke his leg.

AUNT SPONGE: [*Hopefully*] Or his neck, maybe?

AUNT SPIKER: Just *wait* till I get my hands on him. [*Waving her cane*] He'll never want to stay out all night again by the time *I've* finished with him. Good gracious me! What's that awful noise?

AUNT SPONGE: Spiker, I know this sounds silly, but I ... it ... looks as if the fence is breaking ... and ... the Peach is ... the Peach is ...

AUNT SPIKER: Are you ill, Sponge? Are you? *Are you?* You must be ... [SPIKER *notices the Peach moving towards them*] Oh, no! It ... can't ... be ...

AUNT SPONGE: *Move*, Spiker! Out of my way!

AUNT SPIKER: Shove off, Sponge! Me first!

BOTH: *No, no, no! Stay away!* [*Thumping sound*] [SPIKER *and* SPONGE *disappear backstage by slipping through the slit in the curtain – then thumping sound*]

NARRATOR: I wonder what that noise was? Well, anyway, you'll never believe it, but the Giant Peach is still moving. It's rolling and bouncing down the steep slope at a terrific pace. It's going faster and faster and faster, and the crowds of people who were climbing up the hill have suddenly caught sight of it plunging down upon them. They're screaming and scattering to the right and left. It's just knocked over a telegraph pole and flattened two parked cars. It's rushing madly across about twenty fields. Just look at those cows and sheep and horses and pigs stampeding in all directions. Hey, you would scatter too, if the Giant Peach were coming down on you. Wouldn't you? Oh, dear . . . it's rolling right through that village. I don't believe it, but it just went crashing through one of the giant walls of the Wonka-Bucket Chocolate Factory. In fact, there's now a great river of warm, melted chocolate flowing through every street in the village. Will it ever stop? But then, why should it? A round object will always keep on rolling as long as it is on a downhill slope. But wait! There's the sea! Surely the Peach and all its occupants aren't going to end up there? But then, what's to stop it? I know James wanted to visit the seaside, but somehow I don't think that's what he had in mind. It's heading for those towering white cliffs that are the most famous in the whole of England. They're hundreds of feet high. Below them, the sea is deep and cold and hungry. Many ships and men have been swallowed up and lost forever on this part of the coast. The Peach is now only a hundred yards away from the cliff – now fifty – now twenty – now ten – now five – . . . *It's gone over! Down . . . Down . . . Down*

... *Down* ... SMACK!!! [*Tape recording of some-one diving into water; otherwise, something dropped in water can be amplified by using the microphone*] What a colossal splash! Wow! It sank like a stone! *Wait!* I ... think ... I ... see ... yes ... yes ... I ... see something coming ... yes ... yes ... *look over there*!!!

[*Points to auditorium floor in front of stage*]

*End of Scene 3*

## SCENE 4

*Action now takes place on auditorium floor directly in front of the stage. The reason for this is that, when everyone climbs to the top of the Peach, characters can climb to the stage, giving the impression that they are on top. Peach-light is now on, encompassing all characters inside. Characters act all shook up.*

CENTIPEDE: Let's have some light!

OLD-GREEN-GRASSHOPPER: Yes! Light! Give us some light, Glow-worm!

JAMES: Glow-worm? I never met a Glow-worm in here!

CENTIPEDE: That's because he was up on the slimy ceiling, the lazy beast. Although, now that you mention his name, he really doesn't look like much of a worm, does he?

GLOW-WORM: [*Lazily*] I . . . am . . . not . . . a . . . worm . . ! I . . . am . . . not . . . a . . . *he* . . . either! I am simply a lady firefly, without wings!

CENTIPEDE: Big deal! Big deal! Come on, give us some more light!

GLOW-WORM: I'm *trying*! I'm doing my best. Please be patient. [*Change colour filter on spotlight to whatever colour you wish* GLOW-WORM *to give off*] There!

CENTIPEDE: *Some great journey!* [*Limping across the room*]

EARTHWORM: I shall *never* be the same again!

LADYBIRD: Nor I! It's taken *years* off my life!

OLD-GREEN-GRASSHOPPER: But my dear friends! [*Trying to be cheerful*] We are *there*!

SPIDER: Where? Where is *there*?

OLD-GREEN-GRASSHOPPER: I don't know, but I'll bet it's somewhere good.

EARTHWORM: [*Gloomily*] We're probably at the bottom of a coal mine.

OLD-GREEN-GRASSHOPPER: Perhaps we are in the middle of a beautiful country full of songs and music.

JAMES: Or near the seaside, with lots of other children down on the sand for me to play with!

LADYBIRD: Pardon me, but . . . am . . . I . . . wrong . . . in thinking that we seem to be bobbing up and down?

SPIDER: *Bobbing* up and down? What on earth do you mean?

OLD-GREEN-GRASSHOPPER: You're still dizzy from the journey. Is everybody ready to go upstairs now and take a look around?

ALL: Yes, yes! Come on! Let's go!

CENTIPEDE: I *refuse* to show myself out of doors in my bare feet. I *have* to get my boots on again first.

EARTHWORM: For heaven's sake, let's not go through all that nonsense again.

LADYBIRD: Let's *all* lend the Centipede a hand and get it over with. Come on.

SPIDER: While you're doing that, I'll weave a ladder to help us get out.
     [*Everyone crowds around* CENTIPEDE *and acts as if they are putting his shoes on*]

ALL: Okay, we're done! Here we go, boys! The Promised Land! I can't wait to see it!
     [*Everyone climbs up onto the stage, as if they are now on top of the Peach, which is really the top of the beam of light. Remove coloured filter from the spotlight to restore outside of Peach effect*]

CENTIPEDE: But this is *impossible*!

LADYBIRD: I *told* you we were bobbing up and down!

JAMES: We're in the middle of the sea!

ALL: But where are the fields? Where are the woods? Where is England?

OLD-GREEN-GRASSHOPPER: Ladies and gentlemen [*Trying very hard to keep the fear and disappointment out of his voice*], I am afraid that we find ourselves in a rather awkward situation.

EARTHWORM: *Awkward!* We are finished! I may be blind, you know, but that much I can see quite clearly!

CENTIPEDE: Off with my boots! I cannot swim with my boots on!

LADYBIRD: I can't swim at all!

GLOW-WORM: Nor can I!

SPIDER: Nor I!

JAMES: But you won't *have* to swim. We are floating beautifully. And sooner or later a ship is bound to come along and pick us up.
  [*They all stare at him in amazement*]

ALL: [*Except* JAMES] Are you sure we're not sinking?

JAMES: Of course I'm sure. Go and look for yourselves.
  [*They all run over to what is the rim of the spotlight, and look down at the water below*]

OLD-GREEN-GRASSHOPPER: The boy is quite right! We are floating beautifully. Now we must all sit down and keep perfectly calm. Everything will be all right in the end.

EARTHWORM: What absolute nonsense! Nothing is ever all right in the end, and well you know it!

LADYBIRD: Poor Earthworm. [*Whispering to* JAMES] He loves to make everything into a disaster. He hates to be happy.

EARTHWORM: If this Peach is not going to sink, and if we are not going to be drowned, then every one of us is going to *starve* to death instead!

CENTIPEDE: By golly, he's right! For once he is right!

EARTHWORM: Of course. I'm always right! We shall get thinner and thinner and thirstier and thirstier. I am dying already. I am slowly shrivelling up for want of food. Personally, I would rather drown.

JAMES: But you must be *blind*!

EARTHWORM: How cruel! You know very well I'm blind. There's no need to rub it in.

JAMES: I didn't mean that. I'm sorry. But can't you *see* that —

EARTHWORM: *See?* How can I see if I am blind?

JAMES: [*Acting frustrated*] Can't you *realize* that we have enough food here to last us for weeks and weeks?

ALL: [*Except* JAMES] Where? Where?

JAMES: Why, the Peach, of course! Our whole ship is made of food!

ALL: [*Except* JAMES] Jumping Jehoshophat! We never thought of that!

OLD-GREEN-GRASSHOPPER: My dear James, I don't know what we'd do without you. You are so clever.

EARTHWORM: You must be crazy! You can't eat the ship! It's the only thing that is keeping us up!

CENTIPEDE: We shall starve if we don't!

EARTHWORM: And we shall drown if we do!

OLD-GREEN-GRASSHOPPER: Oh dear, oh dear, now we're worse off than before!

JAMES: You can eat all you want. It would take us weeks and weeks to make any sort of a dent in this enormous Peach! Surely you can see that?

OLD-GREEN-GRASSHOPPER: Good heavens, he's right again!

LADYBIRD: An excellent idea!

CENTIPEDE: What are you looking so worried about, Earthworm? What's the problem?

EARTHWORM: The problem is . . . the problem is . . . well, the problem is that there is no problem!

ALL: [*Except* EARTHWORM, *laughing*] Cheer up, Earthworm! Come and eat!
    [*All begin to act as if they are eating the Peach*]

OLD-GREEN-GRASSHOPPER: *Dee*-licious!

GLOW-WORM: Just fabulous!

LADYBIRD: Oh, my! You know, James, this Peach is even better than those tiny little greenflies that live on rosebushes.

SPIDER: And flies were never as good as this!

CENTIPEDE: *What* a flavour! It's terrific! There's nothing like it! There never has been! And I should know because I personally have tasted all the finest foods in the world! [*He breaks into song*]

I've eaten fresh mudburgers by the greatest cooks there are,
And scrambled dregs and stinkbugs' eggs and hornets stewed in tar,
And pails of snails and lizards' tails,
And beetles by the jar.
(A beetle is improved by just a splash of vine*gar*.)

I'm mad for crispy wasp-stings on a piece of
  buttered toast,
And pickled spines of porcupines. And then a gor-
  geous roast
Of dragon's flesh, well hung, not fresh –
It costs a pound at most
(And comes to you in barrels if you order it by
  post).

For dinner on my birthday shall I tell you what I
  chose:
Hot noodles made from poodles on a slice of garden
  hose –
And a rather smelly jelly
Made of armadillo's toes.
(The jelly is delicious, but you have to hold your
  nose.)

Now comes, I do declare, the burden of my speech:
These foods are rare beyond compare – some are
  right out of reach;
But there's no doubt I'd go without
A million plates of each
For one small mite,
One tiny bite
Of this FANTASTIC PEACH!

ALL: Hurray! Beautiful, Centipede! Hurray! [*Except*
EARTHWORM]

CENTIPEDE: *Look!* Look at that funny thin black thing gliding through the water over there!

SPIDER: There are two of them.

LADYBIRD: There are *lots* of them.

EARTHWORM: [*Worriedly*] What are they?

OLD-GREEN-GRASSHOPPER: Probably some kind of fish, come along to say hello.

EARTHWORM: They're sharks! I'll bet you anything you like that they're sharks and they have come along to eat us up!

CENTIPEDE: What absolute rot! [*Unconvincingly*]

EARTHWORM: I am *positive* they are sharks! I just *know* they are sharks!
    [*Everyone looks very worried and looks down at the sharks*]

CENTIPEDE: Ahem. Just assuming that they *are* sharks, there still can't possibly be any danger if we stay up here . . . is there?

GLOW-WORM: Look! They're all swimming in towards us!

ALL: Go away! Go away, you filthy beasts!

GLOW-WORM: Look at the size of their jaws!

SPIDER: Oh dear, they're attacking! We are finished now! They will eat up the whole Peach and then there'll be nothing left for us to stand on. Then they'll start on us!

LADYBIRD: She is right! We are lost forever!

EARTHWORM: Oh, I don't want to be eaten! [*Wailing*] But they will take me first of all because I am so fat and juicy and I have no bones!

LADYBIRD: Is there *nothing* we can do? [*Appealing to* JAMES] Surely *you* can think of a way out of this!
[*Everyone looks at* JAMES *hopefully*]

SPIDER: Think! [*Frantically*] *Think*, James, *think*!

CENTIPEDE: Come on! Come on, James. There *must* be something we can do!

JAMES: There *is* something that I believe we might try. I'm not saying it'll work . . .

EARTHWORM: Tell us! Tell us quickly!

CENTIPEDE: We'll try anything you say! But hurry, hurry, hurry!

LADYBIRD: Be quiet and let the boy speak! Go on, James!

ALL: [*Except* JAMES] Go on! Go *on*!

JAMES: I . . . I . . . I'm afraid it's no good . . . after all . . . [*Shaking his head*] I'm terribly sorry. I forgot. We don't have any string. We'd need hundreds of yards of string to make this work.

OLD-GREEN-GRASSHOPPER: But my dear boy, that's exactly what we do have! We've got all you want!

JAMES: How? Where?

OLD-GREEN-GRASSHOPPER: The Silkworm! Didn't you ever notice the Silkworm? He's still downstairs!

LADYBIRD: Yes, he never moves! He just lies there sleeping all day long, but we can easily wake him up and make him spin!

SPIDER: And what about me, may I ask? I can spin *just* as well as any Silkworm. What's more, *I* can spin patterns.

JAMES: Can you make enough between you?

SPIDER: As much as you want.

JAMES: And quickly?

SPIDER: Of course! Of course!

JAMES: And would it be strong?

SPIDER: The strongest there is!

CENTIPEDE: But why? What are you going to do?

JAMES: I'm going to lift this Peach clear out of the water!

EARTHWORM: You're mad!

JAMES: It's our only chance.

LADYBIRD: Go on, James. How are you going to do it?

CENTIPEDE: Skyhooks, I suppose. [*Jeeringly*]

JAMES: Seagulls! The place is full of them. Look up there! [*Pointing towards the sky*] I'm going to take a long silk string and I'm going to loop one end of it around a seagull's neck. And then I'm going to tie the other end to the stem of the Peach. [JAMES *points to the Peach stem, which is standing up like a short thick mast in the middle of the stage*] Then I'm going to get another seagull and do the same thing again, then another and another –

ALL: [*Except* JAMES] Ridiculous! Poppycock! Absurd! Balderdash! Madness!

OLD-GREEN-GRASSHOPPER: How can a few seagulls lift an enormous thing like this up into the air, and all of us as well?

JAMES: There is no shortage of seagulls. Look for

yourself. We'll probably need four hundred, five hundred . . . maybe even a thousand . . . I don't know . . . I shall simply go on hooking them up to the stem until we have enough to lift us. It's like balloons. You give someone enough balloons to hold, I mean *really* enough, then up he goes. And a seagull has far more lifting power than a balloon. If only we have the *time* to do it.

EARTHWORM: You're absolutely off your head! How on earth do you propose to get a loop of string around a seagull's neck? I suppose you're going to fly up there yourself and catch it!

CENTIPEDE: The boy's dotty!

LADYBIRD: Let him finish! Go on, James. How *would* you do it?

JAMES: With bait!

GLOW-WORM: Bait! What sort of bait?

JAMES: With a worm, of course. Seagulls love worms, didn't you know that? And, luckily for us, we have here the biggest, fattest, juiciest Earthworm . . .

EARTHWORM: *You can stop right there!*

ALL: [*Except* EARTHWORM *and* JAMES] Go on! Go on!

JAMES: The seagulls have already spotted him. That's

why there are so many of them circling around. But they daren't come down to get him while all the rest of us are standing here. So this is what . . .

EARTHWORM: Stop! Stop, stop, stop! I won't have it! I refuse! I – I – I – I –

CENTIPEDE: My dear Earthworm, you're going to be eaten anyway, so what difference does it make whether it's sharks or seagulls?

EARTHWORM: I won't do it!

OLD-GREEN-GRASSHOPPER: Why don't we hear what the plan is first?

EARTHWORM: I don't give a hoot what the plan is! I'm not going to be pecked to death by a bunch of seagulls!

CENTIPEDE: You will be a martyr. I shall respect you for the rest of my life.

JAMES: But he won't *have* to give his life! Now listen to me. This is what we'll do . . .
[*Everyone huddles together while* JAMES *whispers to them*]

OLD-GREEN-GRASSHOPPER: Why, it's absolutely brilliant!

EARTHWORM: Oh, I shall be pecked to death!

CENTIPEDE: Of course you won't!

EARTHWORM: I will, I know I will! And I won't even be able to see them coming at me because I have no eyes!

> [JAMES *goes over and puts his arm on* EARTHWORM'*s shoulder*]

JAMES: I won't let them *touch* you. I promise I won't! But we've got to hurry! Look down there! Action stations! Jump to it! There's not a moment to lose! All hands below deck except Earthworm!

ALL: [*Except* JAMES *and* EARTHWORM] Yes, yes! Come on! Let's hurry!

JAMES: And you – Centipede! Get that Silkworm to work at once! Tell him to spin as he's never spun before! And you too, Spider! Hurry on down! Start spinning!

> [*Everyone that is going down into the Peach goes down the front of the stage, the spotlight is turned off, and the curtain closed*]

*End of Scene 4*

*As the curtain opens, many strings or threads are seen coming either from above or from high off stage down to the stem.* JAMES *is seen tying the last one that is necessary to the stem. Spotlight on. Others are 'below' — not on stage except for* EARTHWORM, *who is half on stage and half off (in hole) being held by* OLD-GREEN-GRASSHOPPER *and* LADY-BIRD.

JAMES: This is the five-hundred-and-second seagull. I think that this one will do it!

EARTHWORM: [*Whining*] Oh, I don't like this at all! Hurry, James!

CENTIPEDE: Quiet down, Earthworm! You should be thankful that you are still alive!

SPIDER: All because James had such a clever idea.

OLD-GREEN-GRASSHOPPER: Yes, I marvel at him. Just think . . . capturing seagulls by using bait. Yes . . . it is a splendid idea.

EARTHWORM: Not if you're the bait!

JAMES: It's working! I can feel us lifting! Look everyone! Come on up! It's working! It's working!

ALL: Oh, isn't it beautiful!

EARTHWORM: What a marvellous feeling! And I'm not hurt!

LADYBIRD: You were very brave, Earthworm.

CENTIPEDE: Good-bye, sharks!

SPIDER: Oh boy, this is the way to travel!

LADYBIRD: Why, you can almost see forever, from up here.

CENTIPEDE: How can you see . . .?

JAMES: Oh, look! There's a ship below us!

OLD-GREEN-GRASSHOPPER: It looks like a big one.

LADYBIRD: It's got three funnels.

CENTIPEDE: You can even see the people on the decks.

SPIDER: Let's wave to them. Do you think they can see *us*?

> [*While waving, everyone goes into frozen-action position while the* NARRATOR *speaks about the ship below. People on the ship are located on the floor in front of the stage, also in frozen-action position until the* NARRATOR *finishes*]

NARRATOR: What an adventure! Can you believe it?

Wow! Now neither James nor any of the others knows it, but the ship that is passing beneath them is actually the *Queen Mary*, sailing out of the English Channel on her way to America. And on the bridge of the *Queen Mary*, the astonished Captain is standing with a group of his officers, all of them gaping at the great round ball hovering overhead.

CAPTAIN: I don't like it!

FIRST OFFICER: Nor do I, Sir.

SECOND OFFICER: Do you think it's following us?

CAPTAIN: I tell you, I don't like it!

FIRST OFFICER: It could be dangerous!

CAPTAIN: That's it! It's a secret weapon! [*Jumping up and down*] Holy cats! Send a message to the Queen at once! The country must be warned! And give me my telescope! [*Looking through telescope*] There are birds everywhere! The whole sky is teeming with birds! What in the world are *they* doing? And wait! Wait a second! There are *people* on it! I can see them moving! There's a – a – do I have this darned thing focused properly? [*Adjusting and hitting telescope*] It looks like a little boy in short trousers! Yes, I can distinctly see a little boy in short trousers standing up there! And there's a –

there's – there's – a – a – a – a sort of *giant lady-bird*!

FIRST OFFICER: Now just a minute, Captain!

CAPTAIN: And a *colossal green grasshopper*!

FIRST OFFICER: Captain! Captain, *please*!

CAPTAIN: And a *mammoth spider*!

SECOND OFFICER: [*Whispering to the* FIRST OFFICER] Oh dear, he's been at the whisky again.

CAPTAIN: [*Screaming*] And an *enormous* – a *simply enormous centipede*!

FIRST OFFICER: Call the ship's doctor! The captain is not well! Get help, *quickly*! [*To the* SECOND OFFICER]

SECOND OFFICER: But, look! It's disappeared into those thick clouds! Now we'll never see it again!

FIRST OFFICER: Never mind that! The Captain has flipped his lid!! He's popped his cork!! I'm the Captain now! Get him off the bridge! Take him below! He's sick! Sick! Sick! *Sick!*

> [*All lights are out as the boat and crew leave the auditorium*]

*End of Scene 5*

## SCENE 6

*Peach spotlight is again put on and everything seems fine as they float through the sky.*

EARTHWORM: I wonder where we'll finish up this time.

CENTIPEDE: Who cares? Seagulls always go back to the land sooner or later.

JAMES: Wow! Didn't it seem as if the people on that ship really got excited when they saw us? But then, I suppose we probably did appear a little peculiar.

LADYBIRD: What do you mean, James?

JAMES: Well . . . what I mean is . . . is . . . is . . .

OLD-GREEN-GRASSHOPPER: What he means is that we all look mighty strange to human beings. And why wouldn't we? After all, they have their ears attached to the sides of their heads.

JAMES: Doesn't everybody?

ALL: [*Except* JAMES] Ha . . . ha . . . ha . . . ha . . .

OLD-GREEN-GRASSHOPPER: Where, for example, do you think that I keep my ears?

JAMES: I . . . don't . . . know.

OLD-GREEN-GRASSHOPPER: Right here. One on each side of my tummy.

EARTHWORM: And I swallow soil!

LADYBIRD: And without charging a penny, I gobble up all the nasty little insects that are gobbling up all the farmers' crops. I am the farmers' best friend.

JAMES: I think you're wonderful. It seems that almost *everyone* around here is loved! How nice this is!

CENTIPEDE: Not me! I am a pest and I'm proud of it! Oh, I am such a shocking, dreadful pest!

EARTHWORM: Hear, hear.

JAMES: But what about you, Spider? Aren't you also much loved in the world?

SPIDER: Oh . . . no . . . I am not loved at all. And yet I do nothing but good. All day long I catch flies and mosquitoes in my webs. I am a decent person.

JAMES: I know you are.

SPIDER: It is very unfair the way spiders are treated. Why, only last week your own horrible Aunt Sponge flushed my poor dear father down the plughole in the bath. I watched the whole thing from a corner up in the ceiling. It was ghastly.

JAMES: But isn't it unlucky to kill a spider?

CENTIPEDE: Of course it's unlucky to kill a spider! Look what happened to Aunt Sponge after she'd done that! *Bump!* We all felt it, didn't we, as the Peach went over her?

SPIDER: It was very satisfactory. Will you sing us a song about it, please?

CENTIPEDE:

Aunt Sponge was terrifically fat,
And tremendously flabby at that.
Her tummy and waist
Were as soggy as paste –
It was worse on the place where she sat!

So she said, 'I must make myself flat.
I must make myself sleek as a cat.
I shall do without dinner
To make myself thinner.'
But along came the Peach!
Oh, the beautiful Peach!
And made her far thinner than that!

SPIDER: That was very nice. Now sing one about Aunt Spiker.

CENTIPEDE: With pleasure. [*Grinning*]

> Aunt Spiker was thin as a wire,
> And as dry as a bone, only drier.
> She was so long and thin
> If you carried her in
> You could use her for poking the fire!

> 'I must do something quickly,' she frowned.
> 'I want *fat*. I want pound upon pound!
> I must eat lots and lots
> Of marshmallows and chocs
> Till I start bulging out all around.

> 'Ah, yes,' she announced, 'I have sworn
> That I'll alter my figure by dawn!'
> Cried the Peach with a snigger,
> '*I'll* alter your figure –'
> And ironed her out on the lawn!
> [*Everyone claps and shouts glad cheers*]

LADYBIRD: Bbbbrrrrrr . . . It's getting colder.

SPIDER: And darker. Why don't we all go down below and keep warm until tomorrow morning?

OLD-GREEN-GRASSHOPPER: No! I think that would be very unwise. It will be safer if we all stay up here through the night and keep watch. Then, if anything happens, we shall be ready for it.

NARRATOR: Well . . . I see that James Henry Trotter and his companions are crouched close together to keep warm. Little do they know what still lies ahead. Oh dear, it scares even me. Well . . . anyway, to get on with the story . . . there is not a sound anywhere. Listen how quiet it is. The Giant Peach is swaying gently from side to side, quietly, softly . . . not at all like aeroplanes that roar through the sky, driving whatever might be lurking secretly up there in the great cloud-mountains back into the cover of the clouds. That is why people who travel in aeroplanes never see anything . . . But the Peach . . . ah, yes . . . the Peach makes no noise at all as it floats along. Wait! . . . Ssssshh . . . Be quiet. There! Over there! Do you see them? I think our travellers are about to, any second . . .

OLD-GREEN-GRASSHOPPER: James, look! What are *those* things?

LADYBIRD: Oooooooooooooh! I don't like this at all!

JAMES: Ssshh! Don't let them hear you! They must be . . . Cloud-Men!

ALL: [*except* JAMES] *Cloud-Men!* Oh dear, oh dear!

EARTHWORM: I'm glad I'm blind and can't see them, or I would probably scream.

SPIDER: I hope they don't turn around and see *us*.

OLD-GREEN-GRASSHOPPER: But what are they *doing*?

JAMES: It seems as if they are reaching out and grabbing handfuls of cloud, rolling them in their fingers, and turning them into large white marbles. There's a huge pile of marbles.

CENTIPEDE: They must be absolutely mad! There's nothing to be afraid of here!

JAMES: Listen! They're singing something! And they're shovelling the marble-like things over the side of the cloud, into space.

CLOUD-MEN:
Down they go!
Hail and snow!
Freezes and sneezes and noses will blow!

JAMES: It's *hailstones*! They've been making hailstones and now they are showering them down onto the people in the world below! They're probably practising for the winter.

CENTIPEDE: That's ridiculous! This is summertime.

You don't have hailstones in summertime. I don't believe it! [*Shouting*]

ALL: [*Except* CENTIPEDE] Ssshh!

JAMES: For heaven's sake, Centipede, don't make so much noise.

CENTIPEDE: [*Roaring with laughter*] Those imbeciles couldn't hear anything! They're deaf as door-knobs! You watch! [*Yelling as loud as he can*] Idiots! Nincompoops! Half-wits! Blunderheads! What are you doing over there! Dummies!
   [CLOUD-MEN *begin jumping around in a fit of anger, but do nothing*]

EARTHWORM: Now you've done it, you loathsome pest!

CENTIPEDE: [*Shouting*] *I'm* not frightened of *them*! [*He dances around and makes insulting signs at the* CLOUD-MEN]

JAMES: Look out! Quick! Lie down flat on the deck! They're throwing hailstones at us!
   [*The* CLOUD-MEN *are angry and making noises, as well as throwing hailstones*]

CENTIPEDE: Ow! Ow! Stop! Stop! Stop!

JAMES: Quickly! Down the tunnel or we'll all be wiped out!

[*Everyone makes a rush for the front of the stage and goes down onto the auditorium floor as if safely inside the Peach. Spotlight filter can be altered here. Curtain closes*]

CENTIPEDE: I'm a wreck! I am wounded all over!

EARTHWORM: It serves you right!

JAMES: Listen! I do believe they're not hitting us any more!

OLD-GREEN-GRASSHOPPER: We've left them behind!

LADYBIRD: The seagulls must have pulled us away out of danger!

SPIDER: Hooray! Let's go up and see!
          [JAMES *goes up first and looks around*]

JAMES: It's all clear! I can't see them anywhere!

*End of Scene 6*

*Everyone climbs back up onto the Peach.*

LADYBIRD: How fast we are going all of a sudden! I wonder why?

JAMES: I don't think the seagulls like this place any better than we do. I imagine they want to get out of it as soon as they can. They got a bad fright out of that hailstone-throwing experience we just had.

NARRATOR: Yes, faster and faster fly the seagulls, skimming across the sky at a tremendous pace, with the Peach trailing out behind them. Cloud after cloud goes by on either side, all of them ghostly white in the moonlight, and several more times during the night the travellers catch glimpses of Cloud-Men moving around on the tops of these clouds, working their sinister magic upon the world below. They even pass a snow machine in operation, with the Cloud-Men turning the handle and a blizzard of snowflakes blowing out of the great funnel above. They see huge drums being used for making thunder. They see frost factories and wind producers and, deep in the hollow of a large billowy cloud, something that can only be a Cloud-Men's city. Just before dawn, they hear a soft *whooshing* noise above their heads and they glance up to see an immense grey bat-like creature swooping down towards them out of the dark. It circles round and round the Peach, flapping its great wings slowly in the moonlight and staring at the travellers. Then it utters a series of long, high cries and flies off again into the night. How terrifying! They all sit motionless. Fearfully, they sit in silence, waiting for the sun, and watching it as it comes up slowly over the rim of the horizon for a new day.

[*This is an ideal place to use a mixture of footlights and overhead lights to create the 'brand-new day' feeling. They all slowly get to their feet to stretch*]

CENTIPEDE: Look! There's land below!

ALL: [*Except* EARTHWORM] He's right! Hooray! Hooray!

GLOW-WORM: It looks like streets and houses.

SPIDER: But how enormous it all is!

LADYBIRD: But what tremendous tall buildings! I've never seen anything like *them* before in England.

OLD-GREEN-GRASSHOPPER: This couldn't possibly be England!

SPIDER: Then where is it?

JAMES: You know what those buildings are? [*Jumping up and down with excitement*] Those are skyscrapers! This must be America! And that, my friends, means that we have crossed the Atlantic Ocean overnight!

OLD-GREEN-GRASSHOPPER: You don't mean it!

CENTIPEDE: It's incredible! It's unbelievable!

EARTHWORM: It's not possible!

CENTIPEDE: Oh, I've always dreamed of going to America! I had a friend once who –

EARTHWORM: Be quiet! Who cares about your friend? The thing we've got to think about now is *how on earth are we going to get down to earth*?

LADYBIRD: Ask James!

JAMES: I don't think that should be so very difficult. All we'll have to do is cut loose a few seagulls. Not too many, mind you, but just enough so that the others can't *quite* keep us up in the air. Then down we shall go, slowly and gently, until we reach the ground. Centipede will bite through the strings for us one at a time.

CENTIPEDE: My goodness, I've forgotten to polish

my boots! Everyone must help me to polish my boots before we arrive!

EARTHWORM: Oh, for heaven's sake! Can't you ever stop thinking about –

[EARTHWORM *is interrupted by a sudden whoosh!*]

SPIDER: What is that?

JAMES: It looks like a plane. It came shooting out of that cloud over there. Wait! Oh, *no*! It's unbelievable! It ... it ... it sliced right through every single one of the silken strings, as it went by!

EARTHWORM: We're falling!

CENTIPEDE: Help!

SPIDER: Save us!

LADYBIRD: We are lost!

OLD-GREEN-GRASSHOPPER: This is the end!

EARTHWORM: James! Do something, James! You've always had the answer before! Quickly, do something!

JAMES: I wish I had the answer. I can't help! I'm sorry! Shut your eyes everybody! It won't be long now!!! . . .

[*Spotlight is turned off and the curtain is closed*

*quickly. After the curtain closes, make a loud whump noise into the microphone, which has been moved backstage after the last* NARRATOR *part*]

*End of Scene 7*

## SCENE 8

*Curtain opens slowly. A large point is seemingly sticking right through the middle of the Peach, as the prop is sitting in the middle of the floor or middle of the spotlight. Everyone is still sitting on the Peach with their eyes closed, expecting to die.*

CENTIPEDE: Good-bye, everybody! Good-bye, Lady-bird! Good-bye . . . Earthworm! I'm sorry that I always picked on you . . . even though you are as blind as a bat . . .

EARTHWORM: Centipede! I ought to . . . oh . . . never mind . . . good-bye, Centipede! I . . . I'm positive you weren't all bad . . .

ALL: [*Except* JAMES] It's the end! I know it is! We're dead! We've had it!

    [JAMES *is looking around in disbelief*]

JAMES: I . . . I . . . I . . . don't believe it! We're not dead!

ALL: [*Except* JAMES] We're not? [*Looking up and around*] We're not dead? . . . We're not! Hooray! Hooray! We're alive!

OLD-GREEN-GRASSHOPPER: But how? Where are we, James?

JAMES: I know it's hard to believe, but I think we've landed on the needle of the Empire State Building!

CENTIPEDE: You're kidding!

EARTHWORM: How will we get down?

JAMES: Don't worry! They'll get us down!

SPIDER: James, why are all those people hanging out of windows cheering us?

LADYBIRD: And all of those people down there on the street are waving madly.

GLOW-WORM: Maybe they think we're heroes.

JAMES: You know, I think you may be right. They think we're heroes! [*Everyone goes into frozen-action positions*]

NARRATOR: [*In front of stage*] James was right! Everyone on the Peach is now looked upon as a hero ... especially James. They were all brought down in five minutes and escorted to the steps of City Hall, where the Mayor of New York made a speech of welcome. And while he was doing this, one hundred steeplejacks, armed with ropes

and ladders and pulleys, swarmed up to the top
of the Empire State Building and lifted the Giant
Peach off the spike and lowered it to the ground.
The Mayor decided that there just had to be a
ticker-tape parade for these wonderful visitors. A
procession was formed, and in the leading car
(which was an enormous open limousine) sat
James and all his friends. Next came the Giant
Peach itself. Men with cranes and hooks had
quickly hoisted it onto a very large truck, and
there it now sat, looking just as huge and proud
and brave as ever. There was, of course, a bit of
a hole in the bottom of it where the spike of the
Empire State Building had gone in, but who
cared about that – or indeed about the peach
juice that was dripping out of it onto the street?
Behind the Peach, skidding about all over the
place in the peach juice, came the Mayor's limousine, and behind that were about twenty other
limousines carrying all the important people of
the City. And the crowds went wild with excitement. They cheered! They yelled! They screamed
and clapped! They tossed bits of white paper and
ticker-tape at James and his friends, who were
standing up in their car waving as they went by.
Then a rather curious thing happened. A little
girl in a red dress ran out from the crowd and
shouted 'Oh, James, James! Could I *please* have

just a tiny taste of your marvellous Peach?'
'Help yourself!' James shouted back. 'Eat all you
want! It won't keep forever, anyway!' Needless to
say, that was the beginning of the end for our
splendid Giant Peach. Children came from
everywhere! They jumped up onto the truck and
swarmed like ants all over the Giant Peach,
eating and eating to their hearts' content. More
and more boys and girls came running from all
directions to join the feast. Soon, there was a trail
of children a mile long chasing after the Peach.
It was really a fantastic sight. To some people it
looked as though the Pied Piper of Hamelin had
suddenly descended upon New York. And to
James, who had never dreamed that there could
be so many children as this in the world, it was
the most marvellous thing that had ever
happened. By the time the procession was over,
the whole gigantic fruit had been completely
eaten up, and only the big brown stone in the
middle, licked clean and shiny by ten thousand
eager little tongues, was left standing on the
truck. And thus the journey ended. But the
travellers lived on. Every one of them became
rich and successful in the new country. The
Centipede was made Vice-President-in-Charge-
of-Sales of a high-class firm of boot and shoe
manufacturers. The Earthworm, with his lovely

pink skin, was employed by a company that made women's face creams to do commercials on television. The Silkworm and Spider, after they had been taught to make nylon thread instead of silk, set up a factory together and made ropes for tightrope walkers. The Glow-worm became the light inside the torch on the Statue of Liberty, and thus saved a grateful City from having to pay a huge electricity bill every year. The Old-Green-Grasshopper became a member of the New York Symphony Orchestra, where his playing was greatly admired. The Ladybird, who had been haunted all her life by the fear that her house was on fire and her children all gone, married the Head of the Fire Department and lived happily ever after. And as for the enormous peach stone – it was set up permanently in a place of honour in Central Park and became a famous monument. But it was not only a famous monument. It was also a famous house. And inside the famous house there lived a famous person – *James Henry Trotter* himself. And all you had to do any day of the week was to go and knock upon the door, and the door would always be opened to you, and you could always ask James to tell and tell again the story of his adventures on the Peach. In fact, James thought it would be nice if one day he sat down and wrote

it as a story for everyone to know. So he did.
And THAT is what you have just seen.

[*Curtain*]

## SOME SUGGESTIONS FOR STAGING

1 Whenever the Narrator speaks, frozen-action positions can be effectively used.

2 The strings for the seagulls – to high side of stage – suggest in which direction the Peach is travelling.

3 The Little-Old-Man can recognizably reappear as the power-hungry First Officer in the boat scene to add even more mystique to his already mysterious role.

4 Instead of using a spotlight to portray the Peach, one could possibly use an inflated material or even build a peach-appearing platform. While both of these could be done, neither is as functional as the spotlight method.

5 Narrator should have a separate spotlight at all times. A filmstrip projector is acceptable.

6 All houselights in the auditorium should be out for the duration of the play.

7 All costuming can be done with painted card-

board or things sewn together. Sheets can be used for Cloud-Men.

8   Very little scenery is essential for this play. Anything added is up to you. Do only that which will enhance and not take away from the action.

*Old-Green-Grasshopper*

Take a large box, cut one side and spread it out. The box should be at least 1.5 metres in width and 1.5 metres in length when spread out.

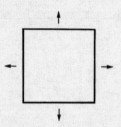

Fold the box in thirds and draw on the body shape. Cut off the outside area.

Use the left-over portion by the wings to make the front feet.

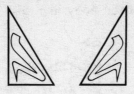

Paint the front legs black, cut them out, and attach them to the folded body.

Using a small box or scrap cardboard, make two identical wings, paint them orange, cut them out, and attach them to the folded body.

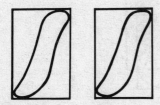

Paint the rest of the body like this:

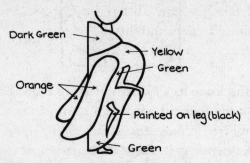

By attaching a couple of cardboard handles to the inside of the body with paper fasteners, you can give the person playing the part some control of his costume. Additional straps or string will help to keep it on.

*Spider*

Take a large box, cut one side and spread it out. The box should be almost the same length or height as the person wearing it. Draw in the Spider and paint it black. Once dry, cut it out and put holes in it where you could insert string or straps to keep it on.

The Spider should be on the person's back and should also be painted black on the reverse side, as part of the reverse side will be visible to the audience. One of the legs can always be gripped (on both sides) for additional stability.

*Ladybird*

Take a large box, cut one side and spread it out. The box should be almost the same length or height as the person wearing it. Draw in the ladybird and paint it bright red. When dry, add black spots at random. When the spots are dry, cut it out and put holes in it where you could insert string or straps to keep it on securely.

The Ladybird should be on the person's back and should also be painted red on the reverse side, as part of the reverse side will be visible to the audience.

*Centipede*

Take a large box, cut one side and spread it out. The box should be almost the same length or height as the person wearing it. Draw in the Centipede and paint it a wild bright colour such as yellow. When dry, cut it out and put holes in it where you could insert string or straps to keep it on securely.

The Centipede should be on the person's back, and a bright colour should also be painted on the reverse side, as part of the reverse side will be visible to the audience. Because of the many legs, socks could be fastened to each 'foot' to add humour and effect.

### Glow-worm, Earthworm, and Silkworm

Glow-worm and Earthworm's costumes should probably be more flowing rather than fixed or rigid. Glow-worm's can simply be a sheet that has been dyed blue and will show up well under certain lighting. It should be fastened around the neck and low on the legs so as to produce a bulging and moving effect.

Earthworm's costume could be done in exactly the same way but perhaps with some vague horizontal striping indicative of a worm.

No costume is necessary for the Silkworm, as the character never speaks and is not even really present in the play. He is referred to as being in certain places but never really involved in the action.

*House*

Take two large boxes, cut one side and spread them out. Attach them end to end for greater length. This can be done by using paper fasteners, strong glue, tape, and staples.

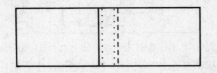

Take other opened-out boxes (or scraps) that are rectangular and add them to the top of the first two boxes by again attaching them with glue, tape, and staples.

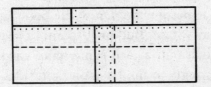

Fold the one big sheet of cardboard into several folds so that it will stand on its own.

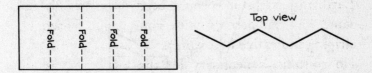

Draw in the look of a house, covering the whole cardboard. Paint it accordingly and cut it out. It

should now stand on its own and be easy to fold up
and move out of the way quickly.

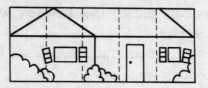

You can use the house when Aunt Sponge and Aunt
Spiker are part of the action.

*Empire State Building spike*
Take a long sheet of cardboard at least 1.5 metres
high and 1 metre wide. Draw the point of the top of
the Empire State Building, paint it with a dark
colour, cut it out, attach some scrap cardboard at a
90 degree angle to the back on both sides to provide
stability, and stand it up.

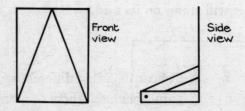

Use it so that the Peach appears to be sitting on top
of it.

*Fence*

Take a piece of cardboard approximately 1 metre wide and 2 metres long (might have to combine and fasten two pieces). Draw a fence on it, paint it an appropriate colour, let it dry, cut it out, and attach some scrap cardboard at a 90 degree angle to the back on both sides to provide stability, and stand it up.

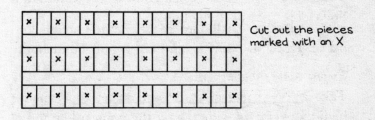

Cut out the pieces marked with an X

To use with house and particularly with the growing Peach. The fence should provide the illusion that it is around the Peach to keep people away from it. The fence could be made bigger if you like.

*Bushes*

Take some pieces of cardboard of different sizes, draw a bush on each, paint them, cut them out, and attach some scrap cardboard at a 90 degree angle to the back on both sides to provide stability, and stand them up.

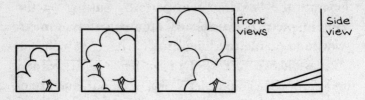

To use with the Little Old Man scene. The man can
hide behind one or several of them.

*Axe*

Take a piece of cardboard that is large enough for
an axe. Draw it, paint it, and cut it out. Paint both
sides.

To be used by James for chopping wood.

*Sea*

Take a couple of good-sized boxes and draw a wavy
line through the middle of each box on all four sides.

Separate the box into two parts by cutting on the
wavy line with a sharp knife. Cut off end flaps.

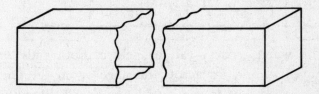

You now have two separate parts. Cut a straight line
down one edge of both parts.

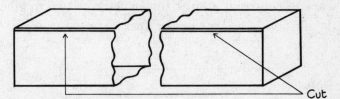

Unfold each half into a long strip.

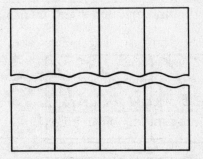

Lay the pieces next to one another, overlapping one
on top of the other. Attach with staples and glue.
Paint blue.

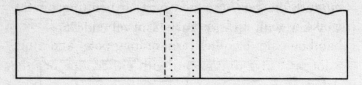

This water scenery can be held at both ends and moved to and fro across the stage or on the floor. You may want to use it with the Peach directly or use it on the auditorium floor with the *Queen Mary*. If you do decide to use it with the *Queen Mary*, you may want to construct a large smoke stack or two to give the illusion of a large ocean liner.

*Sharks*

Take some scraps of cardboard, draw on some sharks' fins (with a base), paint them grey, cut them out, bend over the fin part, and stand them up.

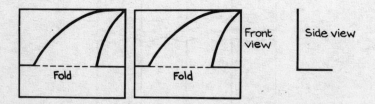

To be used in the scene before the seagulls rescue the Peach. Simply put them around the base of the Peach if you want them, but you don't have to use them.

*String holder and stem*

Make a cone and paint it brown or black. Take a
bamboo pole (or other form of long pole) and attach
a lot of strings to one end with either tape or other
string.

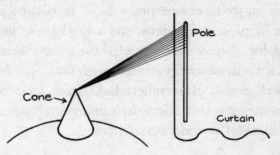

The pole will be used backstage just behind the curtain. The portion with the string attached should be
up in the air. The strings should probably be about
10 metres long, to reach the stem (cone) during the
seagull scene. Then they should be set free from the
cone when the aeroplane 'cuts' them.

## LIGHTING PROCEDURES

These procedures are practical if footlights, upper stage lights, a strobe light, and a spotlight or two are available. If you lack any of these lights, these suggestions will still help you get a general 'feel' for the desired effects. Remember that, while your equipment may not be perfect, by using your imagination you can still provide atmosphere.

SCENE 1    *Spotlight* – for Peach
*Spotlight* – on Narrator, whenever he or she speaks
*Footlights* – red, white, and blue
*Stage Uppers* – red
LIGHTING CHANGE
*Footlights* – red and white off when Narrator begins. Back on when Narrator finishes
*Stage Uppers* – add blue when Narrator finishes
LIGHTING CHANGE
*Footlights* – white and blue off after Narrator mentions first peculiar thing happening to James. Add white again after

James trips with the bag. White off after Aunt Sponge says: 'There really is a peach up there!' White on again after Narrator says: 'James feels that something peculiar is about to happen at any moment.'

*Stage Uppers* – blue off after Narrator mentions first peculiar thing happening to James

SCENE 2    *Spotlight* – for Peach
*Spotlight* – on Narrator, whenever he or she speaks
*Footlights* – red and blue
*Stage Uppers* – red
LIGHTING CHANGE when Aunts walk off
*Footlights* – red off
*Stage Uppers* – red off
*Strobe light* – on after Narrator says: 'He can feel it coming.' Off after James says: 'What's this light . . .?'
LIGHTING CHANGE after James says: 'What's this light . . .?'
*Footlights* – red on now
*Stage Uppers* – red on now

SCENE 3    *Spotlight* – for Peach
*Spotlight* – on Narrator, whenever he or she speaks

*Footlights* – blue
*Stage Uppers* – white

SCENE 4    *Spotlight* – Peach-spot on floor in centre
front at opening of scene. Use blue filter
in spot at this time. Change filter colour
when Glow-worm finally gives off light
*Footlights* – red when everyone goes outside
to top of Peach
*Stage Uppers* – white when everyone goes
outside to top of Peach

SCENE 5    *Spotlight* – Peach-spot should still be Glow-
worm colour as above in Scene 4. Addi-
tional white spot on Narrator when *Queen
Mary* becomes part of Scene. This spotlight is moved to floor on boat and officers
at conclusion of Narrator's remarks. All
lights out at end of Scene

SCENE 6    *Spotlight* – for Peach
*Spotlight* – on Narrator whenever he or she
speaks
*Footlights* – red
*Stage Uppers* – red and white
LIGHTING CHANGE after Ladybird says:
'It's getting colder'

*Footlights* – red and blue. Red off after Narrator
*Stage Uppers* – red and blue. Red off after Narrator

SCENE 7   *Spotlight* – for Peach
*Spotlight* – on Narrator whenever he or she speaks
*Footlights* – blue
*Stage Uppers* – blue
LIGHTING CHANGE when they sight land
*Footlights* – red, white, and blue
*Stage Uppers* – red and blue

SCENE 8   *Spotlight* – for Peach
*Footlights* – red, white, and blue
*Stage Uppers* – red, white, and blue
*Spotlight* – on Narrator at end

Choosing a brilliant book
can be a tricky business...
but not any more

# www.puffin.co.uk

**The best selection of books at your fingertips**

## So get clicking!

Searching the site is easy – you'll find
what you're looking for at the click of a mouse,
from great authors to brilliant books and more!

# Read more in Puffin

For complete information about books available from Puffin – and Penguin – and how to order them, contact us at the appropriate address below. Please note that for copyright reasons the selection of books varies from country to country.

# www.puffin.co.uk

In the United Kingdom: Please write to Dept EP, Penguin Books Ltd, Bath Road, Harmondsworth, West Drayton, Middlesex UB7 ODA

In the United States: Please write to Penguin Putnam Inc., P.O. Box 12289, Dept B, Newark, New Jersey 07101–5289 or call 1–800–788–6262

In Canada: Please write to Penguin Books Canada Ltd, 10 Alcorn Avenue, Suite 300, Toronto, Ontario M4V 3B2

In Australia: Please write to Penguin Books Australia Ltd, P.O. Box 257, Ringwood, Victoria 3134

In New Zealand: Please write to Penguin Books (NZ) Ltd, Private Bag 102902, North Shore Mail Centre, Auckland 10

In India: Please write to Penguin Books India Pvt Ltd, 11 Panscheel Shopping Centre, Panscheel Park, New Delhi 110 017

In the Netherlands: Please write to Penguin Books Netherlands bv, Postbus 3507, NL–1001 AH Amsterdam

In Germany: Please write to Penguin Books Deutschland GmbH, Metzlerstrasse 26, 60594 Frankfurt am Main

In Spain: Please write to Penguin Books S. A., Bravo Murillo 19, 1° B, 28015 Madrid

In Italy: Please write to Penguin Italia s.r.l., Via Felice Casati 20, I–20124 Milano

In France: Please write to Penguin France S. A., 17 rue Lejeune, F–31000 Toulouse

In Japan: Please write to Penguin Books Japan, Ishikiribashi Building, 2–5–4, Suido, Bunkyo-ku, Tokyo 112

In South Africa: Please write to Longman Penguin Southern Africa (Pty) Ltd, Private Bag X08, Bertsham 2013